Prayer

The following Oswald Chambers books are also available from Discovery House Publishers:

Prayer
A Holy Occupation

Oswald Chambers

Edited by HARRY VERPLOEGH

DISCOVERY HOUSE
PUBLISHERS

Prayer: A Holy Occupation
© 1992 by Oswald Chambers Publications Association
Limited. All rights reserved.

Discovery House Publishers is affiliated with RBC
Ministries, Grand Rapids, Michigan.

Discovery House books are distributed to the trade
exclusively by Barbour Publishing, Inc., Uhrichsville,
Ohio.

All Scripture quotations are from the New King James
Version. Copyright © 1979, 1980, 1982 by Thomas
Nelson, Inc., Publishers.

Questions by Julie Ackerman Link

Library of Congress Cataloging-in-Publication Data
Chambers, Oswald, 1874-1917.
    Prayer: a holy occupation/Oswald Chambers.
      p.   cm.
    ISBN 978-0-929239-59-0
    1. Prayer—Christianity. I. Title
BV215.C514 1993
248.3'2—dc20   92-35949
                                    CIP

Printed in the United States of America

08 09 10 11 12 / DP / 18 17 16 15 14

Contents

Introduction

THE JOB OF every Christian is to pray. Plain and simple. Yet we want to do more than simply pray. We want to *do* something important for God; we want to *be* someone important to Him. We want to build; we want to mobilize; we want to show our strength and exert our influence. Prayer seems like such a small thing to do—next to nothing at all in fact.

But that's not what Jesus said. To Him prayer is everything; it's a duty as well as a privilege, a right as well as a responsibility. We use prayer as a last resort; Jesus wants it to be our first line of defense. We pray when there's nothing else we can do; Jesus wants us to pray before we do anything at all.

But most of us would rather spend our time doing something that will get immediate results. We don't want to wait for God to bring about the results in His good time because His idea of "good time" is seldom in sync with ours.

And so we try to help God along. Many times we even try to answer our own prayers. We have the idea that more people will become Christians if we can make God look good to them. So we try to convince them of God's generosity by proving that He answers prayer. If we can just help God spruce up His image a little, we can get more people on His side. And that's what He wants us to do, right?

Wrong. He wants us to pray. Always and about everything. During times of joy as well as sorrow. He wants us to talk *to* Him, not *about* Him. He wants us to talk to Him about unbelievers before we talk to unbelievers about Him.

Prayer is our business, our only business. Prayer is our holy occupation. Plain and simple.

A Holy Occupation
Requires Boldness

IN PRAYER HAVE we learned the wonderful power of that phrase "boldness to enter the Holiest by the blood of Jesus"? It means that we can talk to God as Jesus Christ did, but only through the right of His Atonement. We must never allow the idea that because we have been obedient, because our need is great, because we long for it, therefore God will hear us. There is only one way into the holiest, and that is by the blood of Jesus.[OBH]

Reflection Questions

When was the last time I tried to see an issue from God's perspective rather than ask Him to see it from mine?

SPIRITUAL CERTAINTY IN prayer is God's certainty, not a side-eddy of sanctimoniousness.[DI]

THE ONLY PLATFORM from which the holiest saint on earth is ever heard is the platform mentioned in Hebrews 10:19, we have "boldness to enter the Holiest by the Blood of Jesus." There is no other way. When we come into the presence of God, the human side of our praying makes us realize that if we are ever going to approach God and pray acceptably, it must be by the "piece of God" in us which He has given us.[IYA]

Reflection Questions

How can I be sure I am praying acceptably?

IT IS BECAUSE our Lord Jesus Christ went through the depths of agony to the last ebb in the Garden of Gethsemane, because He went through Calvary, that we can boldly enter the holy place.[IYA]

THERE ARE UNDOUBTEDLY things which present a puzzle. For example, the presentation of the basis of redemption, how am I going to understand whether the redemption covers everything, or only partially covers? Never by reasoning, only by prayer; and as sure as God is God you will get the answer and know of a certainty.[BFB]

Reflection Questions

What prayer of mine do I consider still "unanswered"? If indeed it has been answered without my awareness, how should I change that prayer?

JESUS NEVER MENTIONED unanswered prayer, He had the boundless certainty that prayer is always answered.[MUH]

THE CURE OF uncertainty is a new note of intercessory prayer. The reason for perplexity in meeting the actual occurrences of life is because we are losing face-to-face contact with Jesus Christ through His Cross. We must get back to the place where we are concerned only about facing our own inner souls with Jesus Christ Who searches us right down to the inmost recesses.ᴾᴴ

Reflection Questions

What am I trying to hide from Jesus? How might my life be different if I admitted to myself and to Him that it is there and needs His attention? Will I confess today or continue to procrastinate?

ASKING IN PRAYER is at once the test of three things— simplicity, stupidity, and certainty of God.ᴰᴵ

JESUS SAYS THERE are times when our heavenly Father will appear as if He were a most unnatural father, callous and indifferent. But remember, says Jesus, I have told you—"everyone who asks receives." When we get into spiritual confusion the usual way out is to say we have made a blunder, and we go back instead of forward. "I don't know what to do; I am up against a stone wall." Will you "hang in" to what Jesus said? If there is a shadow on the face of God the Father just now, remain confident that ultimately He will give His clear issue as Jesus said. It is not a question of black or white or right or wrong, of being in communion or out of communion; but a question of God taking us by a way which in the meantime we do not understand.[PH]

Reflection Questions
What is one issue about which God seems indifferent to me? Is my response one of faith or doubt?

Requires Boldness

WE ARE BASED on the platform of reality in prayer by the Atonement of our Lord Jesus Christ. It is not our earnestness that brings us into touch with God, not our devotedness, nor our times of prayer, but our Lord Jesus Christ's vitalizing death; and our times of prayer are evidences of reaction on the reality of redemption, so we have confidence and boldness of access into the Holiest. What an unspeakable joy it is to know that we each have the right of approach to God in confidence, that the place of the Ark is our place, "therefore, brethren, having boldness." What an awe and what a wonder of privilege, *"to enter the Holiest,"* in the perfectness of the atonement *"by the blood of Jesus."* CD Vol. 2

Reflection Questions

What will I do today as an expression of gratitude and praise for the awesome privilege of prayer?

LAUNCH OUT IN reckless belief that the redemption is complete, and then bother no more about yourself, but begin to do as Jesus Christ said—pray for the friend who comes to you at midnight, pray for the saints, pray for all people. Pray on the realization that you are only perfect in Christ Jesus, not on this plea—"O Lord, I have done my best, please hear me." MUH

Reflection Questions
What would "reckless belief"
cause me to do today?

SO MANY OF us limit our praying because we are not reckless in our confidence in God. In the eyes of those who do not know God, it is madness to trust Him, but when we pray in the Holy Spirit we begin to realize the resources of God, that He is our perfect heavenly Father, and we are His children.IYA

NEVER SAY GOD has done what He has not done because it sounds better to say it; never pretend to have an answer when you have not. Jesus said, "Everyone who asks receives"; we say—"I have asked but I have not received." It is because we ask in spiritual confusion. Jesus said to James and John: "You do not know what you ask"; they were brought into fellowship with Jesus Christ's cup and baptism, but not in the way they expected.^{PH}

Reflection Questions
Am I in a state of spiritual confusion?
What am I really asking God for
when I pray?

THE ONLY WAY to get into the relationship of "asking" is to get into the relationship of absolute reliance on the Lord Jesus. "Now this is the confidence that we have in Him."^{DI}

PAUL SAYS, "PRAYING always . . . for all the saints and for me." Do we remember to pray on the ground of our Lord's orders for all who minister in His name? If the apostle Paul earnestly solicited prayer on his behalf that "I may open my mouth boldly to make known the mystery of the gospel," surely it behooves us to remember that this is the key our Lord puts into our hands for all Christian work; not prayer because we are helpless, but prayer because God is almighty.[IYA]

Reflection Questions
What church leader should I stop
grumbling about and start praying for?

WE CAN GET to God as Creator apart from Jesus Christ, but never to God as our Father except through Him. Let us receive this inspired idea of our Lord's into our inmost willing heart, believe it, and pray in the confidence of it.[CD Vol. 2]

Requires Boldness

IF YOU HAVE a gift of prayer, may God wither it up until you learn how to get your prayers inspired by God the Holy Spirit. Do we rely on God, or on our own earnestness when we pray? God is never impressed by our earnestness; we are not heard because we are in earnest, but on the ground of redemption only. We have "boldness to enter the Holiest by the blood of Jesus" and by no other way.^{SSM} ^[SSM]

Reflection Questions

How much of my praying is for myself and how much is for God? How might I change my prayers to make them less self-centered?

OUR IMPORTUNITY MUST be intercessory and the whole power of our intercession lies in the certainty that prayer will be answered.^{CD Vol. 2} ^[CD Vol. 2]

THEREFORE, BROTHERS, HAVING *boldness to enter the Holiest by the blood of Jesus.* Beware of imagining that intercession means bringing our personal sympathies into the presence of God and demanding that He do what we ask. Our approach to God is due entirely to the vicarious identification of our Lord with sin.[MUH]

Reflection Questions

Do my prayers sound like an employee asking for a raise? How should my relationship with God be different from that of an employee?

INTELLECT AND PRAYER are united in the saint in the consciousness of Christ which we share, consequently the consciousness of self-realization is a perversion and a snare.[CD Vol. 2]

A Holy Occupation
Requires Childlikeness

THE MEANING OF intercession is that we see what God is doing, consequently there is an intimacy between the child and the Father which is never impertinent. We must pour into the bosom of God the cares which give us pain and anxiety in order that He may solve for us, and before us, the difficulties which we cannot solve. We injure our spiritual life when we dump the whole thing down before God and say—You do it. That spirit is blind to the real union with God. We must dump ourselves down in the midst of our problems and watch God solve them for us. "But I have no faith"—bring your problems to God and stay with Him while He solves them, then God Himself and the solution of your problems will be for ever your own. If we could see the floor of God's immediate presence, we would find it strewn with the "toys" of God's children who have said—This is broken, I can't play with it any more, please give me another present. Only one in a thousand sits down in the midst of it all and says—I will watch my Father mend this.^{NKW}

Requires Childlikeness

WHATEVER YOU ASK in My name, that I will do. When you pray, remember that it is Jesus Christ who carries out the answer, God hands over this marvelous power to Him. By His Ascension our Lord becomes omniscient, all-wise; have we ever had a glimpse of what that means? The wisdom which He exercised in a limited sphere and in complete dependence upon His Father while on earth, He can now exercise in an unlimited sphere. Get on to the supernatural line, remember that Jesus Christ is omniscient, and He says, "If you ask anything in My name, I will do it."[BSG]

Reflection Questions

What prayer am I trying to answer in my own strength?

THE ONLY ONE who prays in the Holy Ghost is the child, the child-spirit in us, the spirit of utter confidence in God.[IYA]

BY WHAT RIGHT do we become "a royal priesthood"? By the right of the Atonement. Are we prepared to leave ourselves resolutely alone and to launch out into the priestly work of prayer? The continual grubbing on the inside to see whether we are what we ought to be generates a self-centered, morbid type of Christianity, not the robust, simple life of the child of God.ᴹᵁᴴ

Reflection Questions
With whom, or in what situation, do I
need to become less self-centered
and more God-centered?

IN REGARD TO prayer, we are apt to be apologetic and apathetic, complex and confused; yet what a splendid audacity a child has, and that is what our Lord taught us to have.ᶜᴰ ⱽᵒˡ· ²

PRAYER TO US is not practical, it is stupid, and until we do see that prayer is stupid, that is, stupid from the ordinary natural common sense point of view, we will never pray. "It is absurd to think that God is going to alter things in answer to prayer." But that is what Jesus says He will do. It sounds stupid, but it is a stupidity based on His redemption. The reason that our prayers are not answered is that we are not stupid enough to believe what Jesus says.[SSY]

Reflection Questions

Am I willing to be considered stupid by those who don't know Jesus? What difference will it make in my life?

AS LONG AS we are self-sufficient and complacent, we don't need to ask God for anything, we don't want Him; it is only when we know we are powerless that we are prepared to listen to Jesus Christ and to do what He says.[IYA]

AND YOUR FATHER *who sees in secret.* The revelation here is of the free kingdom of love; there is not blind creaturely subjection to a Creator, but the free kingdom in which the one who prays is conscious of limit only through the moral nature of the Father's holiness. It is a revelation of pure joyousness in which the child of God pours into the Father's bosom the cares which give pain and anxiety that He may solve the difficulties. We are not beggars on the one hand or spiritual customers on the other; we are God's children, and we just stay before Him with our broken treasures or our pain and watch Him mend or heal in such a way that we understand Him better.[CD Vol. 2]

*R*eflection *Q*uestions

*Do my prayers sound as if I am one of
God's customers rather than
one of His children?*

IT IS NEVER God's will for us to be dummies or babies spiritually; it is God's will for us to be sons and daughters of God. But He does not prevent us paying the price of being sons and daughters. He makes us sons and daughters potentially, and then sends us out to be sons and daughters actually. Are we prepared to go into the shameless business of prayer? That is, are we prepared to get to the right understanding of God in this matter? We can only get it by one way, not by disputing or controversy, but by prayer. Keep at it. We have no business to remain in the dark about the character of our Father when He has made His character very clear to us.[IYA]

Reflection Questions

Do I get my understanding of God from God Himself or from other people? What does God have to say about Himself that is different from what others say about Him?

WE PRAY PIOUS blather; our will is not in it. And then we say God does not answer. We never asked for anything. "You will ask what you desire," said Jesus. Asking means our will is in it. Whenever Jesus talked about prayer, He put it with the grand simplicity of a child; we bring in our critical temper and say—Yes, but . . . Jesus said, "Ask." But remember that we have to ask of God things that are in keeping with the God whom Jesus Christ revealed.ᴹᵁᴴ

Reflection Questions
Do I know God well enough to know
how He wants me to pray? What will I
do today to get to know Him better?

IF WE ARE asking God to give us experiences, we hurt the Lord. The very questions we ask hurt Jesus because they are not the questions of a child.ᴹᵁᴴ

Requires Childlikeness

WHEN WE PRAY in the Holy Spirit, we bring to God the things that come quite naturally to our minds, and the Holy Spirit, Who intercedes for the saints according to the will of God, enables God to answer the prayer He Himself prays in your bodily temple and mine—that we may be the children of our Father which is in heaven. The Holy Spirit cannot delight in our wisdom; it is the wisdom of God He delights in.[IYA]

Reflection Questions

In what ways do I make my prayers more complicated than God intended them to be?

ARE YOU LONGING after sanctification? Have you such confidence in Jesus that you can pray this prayer, the prayer of a child—"Father, in the Name of Jesus, baptize me with the Holy Spirit and fire until sanctification is made real in my life"?[OBH]

IT IS QUITE true God does not answer some prayers because they are wrong, but that is so obvious that it does not need a revelation from God to understand it. God wants us to stop understanding in the way we have understood and get into the place He wants us to get into, that is, He wants us to know how to rely on Him.[IYA]

Reflection Questions

In what ways do I try to "outsmart" God by trying to determine a formula for getting Him to answer prayer?

THERE IS ONLY one kind of person who can really pray, and that is the childlike saint, the simple, stupid, supernatural child of God; I do mean "stupid." Immediately you try to explain why God answers prayer on the ground of reason, it is nonsense; God answers prayer on the ground of redemption and no other ground.[IYA]

THE GREATEST BARRIER to intercession is that we take ourselves so seriously and come to the conclusion that God is reserved with us; He is not. God has to ignore things we take so seriously until our relationship to Him is exactly that of a child.^{MFL}

Reflection Questions
What things do I take more seriously than God? What can I do to help myself see them as He sees them?

THE NEARER ABRAHAM came to God in his intercession the more he recognized his entire unworthiness: "Indeed now, I who am but dust and ashes have taken upon myself to speak to the Lord." Genuine unworthiness is never shy before God any more than a child is shy before his mother. A child of God is conscious only of his entire dependence upon God.^{NKW}

WHEN WE LIVE in the secret place it becomes impossible for us to doubt God, we become more sure of Him than of anything else. Your Father, Jesus says, is in secret and nowhere else. Enter the secret place, and right in the center of the common round you find God there all the time.ᴹᵁᴴ

Reflection Questions
Am I looking for God in all the wrong places? Where should I be looking instead?

I AM THERE *in the midst of them.* A wonderful picture—a group of our Lord's children around the knees of the heavenly Father, making their requests known in familiarity, in awe and reverence, in simplicity and confidence in Him, and in humble certainty that He is there.ᶜᴰ ⱽᵒˡ. ²

Requires Childlikeness

WHAT A PERSON wants is somewhere to rest his mind and heart, and the only place to rest is in God, and the only way to come to God is by prayer. Much of our prayer has nothing in it; it is not the talk of a child to his Father when he has come up against things or is hurt.BFB

Reflection Questions

Where do I most often go in search of rest when I should be going to God? How much of my praying is empty?

WE GROUSE BEFORE God, we are apologetic or apathetic, but we ask very few things. Yet what a splendid audacity a child has! Our Lord says—"Unless you become as little children." Ask, and God will do.MUH

THERE IS A subtle thing that goes by the name of unworthiness which is petulant pride with God. When we are shy with other people it is because we believe we are superior to the average person and we won't talk until they realize our importance. Prayerlessness with God is the same thing; we are shy with God not because we are unworthy, but because we think God has not given enough consideration to our case, we have some peculiar elements He must be pleased to consider.[IYA]

Reflection Questions
Is my shyness with God like that of an adoring child or a spoiled child?

ONLY A CHILD gets prayer answered; a wise man does not.[MUH]

A Holy Occupation
Requires Communion

GOD IS GOING to judge us by the times when we have been in living communion with Him, not by what we feel like today. God judges us entirely by what we have seen. We are not judged by the fact that we live up to the light of our conscience; we are judged by the Light—Jesus Christ. "I am the light of the world"; and if we do not know Jesus Christ, we are to blame. The only reason we do not know Him is because we have not bothered our heads about Him. Honestly, does it matter to us whether Jesus lived and died, or did anything at all? But there are so many humbugs. There is no counterfeit without the reality. Is Jesus Christ a fraud? We are to be judged by Him. This is the condemnation, that light is come into the world, and men loved the darkness rather than the light. We are not judged by the light we have, but by the light we have refused to accept. God holds us responsible for what we will not look at. A man is never the same after he has seen Jesus. We are judged by our immortal moments, the moments in which we have seen the light of God.^{PH}

THE CONSCIOUS AND the subconscious life of our Lord is explained perhaps in this way. Our Lord's subconscious life was Deity, and only occasionally when He was on earth did the subconscious burst up into His conscious life. The subconscious life of the saint is the Holy Spirit, and in such moments of prayer as are alluded to in Romans 8:26–28, there is an uprush of communion with God into the consciousness of the saint, the only explanation of which is that the Holy Spirit in the saint is communicating prayers which cannot be uttered. CD Vol. 2

Reflection Questions
What can I do to allow the Holy Spirit
room to work in my subconscious?

THE ENEMY DOES all he can against our communion with God, against our solitude with God, he tries to prevent us from "drawing our breath in the fear of the Lord." DI

37

THE TIME A Christian gives to prayer and communion with God is not meant for his natural life, but to nourish the life of the Son of God in him. God engineers the circumstances of His saints in order that the Spirit may use them as the praying house of the Son of God. If you are spiritual the Holy Spirit is offering up prayers in your bodily temple that you know nothing about, it is the Spirit making intercession in you.[BE]

Reflection Questions
What are the spiritual blessings God gives
me? Am I too consumed with the cares of
my natural life to enjoy them?

PRAYER IN DISTRESS dredges the soul. It is a good thing to keep a note of the things you prayed about when you were in distress. We remain ignorant of ourselves because we do not keep a spiritual auto-biography.[OPG]

WHEN THE SPIRIT of God comes in and energizes the spirit of a man, what happens is that he is taken up into the great mystery of the Holy Spirit interceding in him along a particular line. If the Holy Spirit is allowed to dwell in the human spirit He has energized, he will express the unutterable. Think what that means. It means being quickened by the incoming of the Holy Spirit who comes in to dwell supremely, and the amazing revelation is that He intercedes in us, for us, with a tenderness exactly in accordance with the Mind of God.[IYA]

Reflection Questions

How has the knowledge that the Holy Spirit not only lives in me but also prays for me according to the perfect will of God the Father changed my life?

WE CANNOT TALK to God unless we walk with Him when we are not talking.[HGM]

EVERY TIME WE pray our horizon is altered, our attitude to things is altered, not sometimes but every time, and the amazing thing is that we don't pray more. Prayer is a complete emancipation, it keeps us on the spiritual plane. When you are at one with another mind there is a telepathic influence all the time, and when born from above the communion is between God and yourself.[PH]

Reflection Questions

How has my mind been altered by prayer? What thoughts have come to my mind during prayer that might never have occurred to me if I hadn't taken time to pray?

SPECIFIC TIMES AND places and communion with God go together. It is by no haphazard chance that in every age men have risen early to pray.[HGM]

Requires Communion

OUR PRAYERS SHOULD be in accordance with the nature of God, therefore the answers are not in accordance with our nature but with His. We are apt to forget this and to say without thinking that God does not answer prayer; but He always answers prayer, and when we are in close communion with Him we know that we have not been misled.^{CD Vol. 2}

Reflection Questions

What answers to prayer have I been unable to see because I am not in close enough communion with God?

ONE OF THE first lessons learned in the Ministry of the Interior is to talk things out before God in soliloquy—tell Him what you know He knows in order that you may get to know it as He does.^{HGM}

41

THERE ARE CERTAIN times of the day when it not only *seems* easier, but it *is* easier to meet God. If you have ever prayed in the dawn you will ask yourself why you were so foolish as not to do it always; it is difficult to get into communion with God in the midst of the hurly-burly of the day. George MacDonald said that if he did not open wide the door of his mind to God in the early morning he worked on the finite all the rest of the day—"stand on the finite, act upon the wrong." It is not sentiment but an implicit reality that the conditions of dawn and communion with God go together. When the day of God appears there will be no night, always dawn and day. There is nothing of the nature of strain in God's day; it is all free and beautiful and fine.[HGM]

*R*eflection *Q*uestions

When is the best time of day for me to commune with God? Is morning best for everyone?

A Holy Occupation
Requires Concentration

ON THE MOUNT with God, you saw that all power has been given to Jesus in heaven and on earth. Are you going to be skeptical in the valley of humiliation? You have gone to God about the thing that is perplexing you over and over again and nothing has happened. "Why could we not cast it out?" Our Lord never gives an answer to questions of that description, because the answer lies in a personal relationship to Himself. "This kind does not go out except by prayer and fasting," that is, by concentration on God. That is the one purpose for which we are in the world.[LG]

Reflection Questions

If I were to concentrate more on God in my prayers, how might that change the way I see my problems?

CONCENTRATION ON THE part of a Christian is of more importance than consecration.[BE]

44

Requires Concentration

It is at first difficult to learn a new and better way of breathing, consequently we are conscious of it for a time, but it is merely consciousness of what will by habit become an unconscious possession. So in the better and new way of breathing spiritually in prayer, we shall be conscious of forming the habit, but it will soon pass into normal spiritual health.^{CD Vol. 2}

Reflection Questions

Is prayer as natural to me as breathing?
How can I make it less of a conscious act
and more of a natural response
to God in my life?

Get to work and seek, narrow your interests to this one thing. Have you ever really sought God, or have you only given a languid cry to Him after a twinge of moral neuralgia?^{OBH}

IN MENTAL WORK it takes time to gain the victory over wandering thoughts; they do not come necessarily through supernatural agents, but through lack of concentration. Concentration is only learned little by little, and the more impulsive you are, the less concentrated you will be.^{CD Vol. 2}

Reflection Questions

What can I do to improve my spiritual concentration? Would it help if I were to put my thoughts and prayers into writing?

IMPULSE IN ANYONE but a child is dangerous; it is the sign of something unstable and unreliable. Determination means to fix the form of our choice, and God demands that we use this power when we pray. The majority of us waste our time in mere impulses in prayer.^{BP}

Requires Concentration

WE HAVE TO see that we continually work out with concentration and care that which God has worked in, not work our own salvation, but work it out. We have to work out what God works in while we rest resolutely in unshaken faith on the complete and perfect redemption of the Lord Jesus Christ.OBH

Reflection Questions

Am I depending on myself to do what only God can do? Am I depending on God to do what He expects me to do?

THE MAJORITY OF us are unable to fix our thoughts in prayer. We lie all abroad before God and do not rouse ourselves up to lay hold of Him, consequently we have wandering thoughts continually. God will not bring every thought and imagination into captivity; we have to do it, and that is the test of spiritual concentration.MFL

ATMOSPHERE IS NOT only something assimilated, but something we help to produce, and is both subjective and objective. To ask the Spirit of God to take up His abode in the atmosphere of a meeting is not at all unnecessary; the idea of "sacred places" can be easily abused, but it does not follow that there is no such thing as a sacred place. For instance, it is easier to pray in a place used only for prayer than it is to pray in a theater.^{CD Vol. 2}

Reflection Questions
Where is the best place for me to pray?
What place will contribute to
maximum concentration?

IT IS SO difficult to get "quiet," you say. What about the time when you were ill? Oh, it can be done, but you must know how to shut the door.^{CD Vol. 2}

Requires Concentration

THINK OF THE enormous leisure of God! He never is in a hurry. We are in such a frantic hurry. We get down before God and pray, then we get up and say, "It is all done now," and in the light of the glory of the vision we go forth to do the thing. But it is not real, and God has to take us into the valley and put us through fires and floods to batter us into shape, until we get into the condition in which He can trust us with the reality of His recognition of us.ssy

---

Reflection Questions

In what ways does all my activity keep me from concentrating on God? If I spend no quality time with God, how can I know that I am accomplishing what is important to Him?

BEWARE LEST ACTIVITY in proclaiming the Truth should mean a cunning avoidance of spiritual concentration in intercession.DI

DID YOU EVER say anything like this to yourself, "It is so difficult to select a place?" What about the time when you were in love, was it impossible to select a place to meet? No, it was far from impossible; and beware of self-indulgence. Think how long our Lord has waited for you; you have seen Him in your visions, now pray to Him; get a place, not a mood, but a definite material place and resort to it constantly, and pray to God as His Spirit in you will help you. Bring to earth the promised life you have longed for. Curb your impulsive undisciplined wayward nature to His use, and rule your body like a king where now, even in strength and honesty, you walk prey to baser and less spiritual things. Do not say, "If I only had so and so"; you have not got so and so; but we can always do what we want to do if our want to do it is sufficient. CD Vol. 2

Reflection Questions

Is my "want" to pray sufficient to make me pray? If not, why not?

A Holy Occupation
Requires Desire

A GREAT MANY people do not pray because they do not feel any sense of need. The sign that the Holy Spirit is in us is that we realize, not that we are full, but that we are empty. There is a sense of absolute need. We come across people who try us, circumstances that are difficult, conditions that are perplexing, and all these things awaken a dumb sense of need, which is a sign that the Holy Spirit is there.[IYA]

Reflection Questions

How great is my sense of need? What does it tell me about my spirituality?

IF WE ARE ever free from the sense of need, it is not because the Holy Spirit has satisfied us, but because we have been satisfied with as much as we have. "A man's reach should exceed his grasp." A sense of need is one of the greatest benedictions because it keeps our life rightly related to Jesus Christ.[IYA]

Requires Desire

AND WHEN YOU *pray, you shall not be like the hypocrites, For they love to pray standing in the synagogues and on the corners of the streets, that they may be seen by men. Assuredly, I say to you, they have their reward.* Watch your motive; does it arise from a real enchantment? (The word *hypocrites* here is really "play actors.") The main idea in the region of religion is—your eyes upon God, not on men. Do not have as your motive the desire to be known as a praying man. Get an inner chamber in which to pray where no one knows you are praying, shut the door and talk to God in secret. Have no other motive than to know your Father in heaven.ᴹᵁᴴ

Reflection Questions
What are my motives for prayer?

THINK OF THE last thing you prayed about—were you devoted to your desire or to God? Determined to get some gift of the Spirit or to get at God?ᴹᵁᴴ

LORD GOD OMNIPOTENT, how my soul delights to know that you care for sparrows and number the hairs of our heads! Lord, breathe on me till I am in the frame of mind and body to worship You. O Lord, I would seek Your face now, but what avail is my seeking if You reveal not Yourself? Show me Your face, O Lord. Keep me ever seeing You. O Lord, to praise You aright is a great desire of mine, created and fostered by Your Spirit and grace. This morning, O Lord, I praise You for all the past—so wayward on my part, so wonderful and gracious and longsuffering and forgiving and tender and inspiring on Yours.[IYA]

Reflection Questions
When I pray, what conception do I have
in my mind—my need or
Christ's omnipotence?

Requires Desire

THE POINT OF asking is that you may get to know God better. "Delight yourself also in the Lord, and He shall give you the desires of your heart." Keep praying in order to get a perfect understanding of God Himself.[MUH]

Reflection Questions
What have I learned about God this week
as a result of praying?

HAVE YOU EVER asked out of the depths of moral poverty? "If any of you lack wisdom, let him ask of God." But be sure that you do lack wisdom. You cannot bring yourself up against reality when you like.[MUH]

WHEN WE PRAY for others the Spirit of God works in the unconscious domain of their beings that we know nothing about, and the one we are praying for knows nothing about, but after the passing of time the conscious life of the one prayed for begins to show signs of unrest and disquiet. We may have spoken until we are worn out, but have never come anywhere near, and we have given up in despair. But if we have been praying, we find on meeting one day that there is the beginning of a softening in an enquiry and a desire to know something. It is that kind of intercession that does most damage to Satan's kingdom. It is so slight, so feeble in its initial stages, that if reason is not wedded to the light of the Holy Spirit, we will never obey it. And yet it is that kind of intercession that the New Testament places most emphasis on, though it has so little to show for it. It seems stupid to think that we can pray and all that will happen, but remember to Whom we pray. We pray to a God Who understands the unconscious depths of personality about which we know nothing, and He has told us to pray.[IYA]

A Holy Occupation
Requires Discipline

ALL CHRISTIANS WITH any experience at all have had a vision of some fundamental truth, either about the Atonement or the Holy Spirit or sin, and it is at the peril of their souls that they lose the vision. By prayer and determination we have to form the habit of keeping ourselves soaked in the vision God has given.

The difficulty with the majority of us is that we will not seek to apprehend the vision; we get glimpses of it and then leave it alone. "I was not disobedient to the heavenly vision," says Paul.

It is one of the saddest things to see men and women who have had visions of truth but have failed to apprehend them, and it is on this line that judgment comes. It is not a question of intellectual discernment or of knowing how to present the vision to others, but of seeking to apprehend the vision so that it may apprehend us. PS

Reflection Questions
What is the vision God has given me?
What am I doing to be obedient to it?

Requires Discipline

SOAK AND SOAK and soak continually in the one great truth of which you have had a vision; take it to bed with you, sleep with it, rise up in the morning with it, continually bring your imagination into captivity to it, and slowly and surely as the months and years go by God will make you one of His specialists in that particular truth.[PS]

Reflection Questions

What do I expect to accomplish apart from prayer? What am I waiting to "see" before I am willing to obey?

WE ARE ALL Pharisees until we are willing to learn to intercede. We must go into heaven backwards; that phrase means we must grow into doing some definite thing by praying, not by seeing. To learn this lesson of handling a thing by prayer properly is to enter a very severe school. The duty of Christians is not to themselves or to others, but to Christ.[IYA]

THINKING IS THE habit of expressing what moves our spirit. In order to think we must concentrate. Thinking is a purely physical process. No one can tell us how to begin to think, all they can do is to tell us what happens when we do think.

The inattentive, slovenly way we drift into the presence of God is an indication that we are not bothering to think about Him.[MFL]

Reflection Questions

Do my prayers consist only of what I am personally interested in? When I pray, do I think about God or about myself?

INTEREST IS NATURAL, attention must be by effort. One of the great needs of the Christian life is to have a place where we deliberately attend to realities. That is the real meaning of prayer.[RTR]

Requires Discipline

THERE IS A quietism of devotional self-indulgence which takes the place spiritually that loafing does socially. It is easy to call it meditative prayer, but meditation is only attained in actual life by the strenuous discipline of brooding in the center of a subject. A saint endeavors consciously and strenuously to master the technical means of expressing God's life in himself. The place of prayer in the New Testament is just this one of severe technical training in which spiritual sympathies are sustained in unsecular strength, and manifested in the vulgar details of actual life.[CD Vol. 2]

Reflection Questions

Is my prayer life more like a playground or a gymnasium?

IF YOUR CROWD knows you as a man or woman of prayer, they have a right to expect from you a nobler type of conduct than from others.[DI]

THE OBJECTION IS frequently brought forward that it is so difficult to concentrate one's thoughts in prayer. Yet what about the time you were working for that position, or to pass that examination? All our excuses arise from some revealing form of self-indulgence. In the beginning we may clamor for presents and for things, and our Father encourages us in these elementary petitions until we learn to understand Him better; then we begin to talk to Him in free reverent intimacy, understanding more and more His wonderful nature.CD Vol. 2

Reflection Questions
If I could look at myself from God's
perspective, what would I see
as my true needs?

THE WHOLE SOURCE of our strength is receiving, recognizing, and relying on the Holy Spirit.IYA

Requires Discipline

THE REASON WE do not pray is that we do not own Jesus Christ as Master; we do not take our orders from Him. The key to the Master's orders is prayer, and where we are when we pray is a matter of absolute indifference. In whatever way God is engineering our circumstances, that is the duty.[SSY]

Reflection Questions

What are my motives for prayer – to get God to do things my way or to get me to do things His way?

IF WE ARE struggling in prayer it is because the wiles of the Enemy are getting the upper hand and we must look for the cause of it in the lack of discipline in ourselves.[IYA]

THERE ARE SPIRITUAL loafers who are painfully im-
pressionable about "tones" and "moods" and "places,"
and they remind one of the aesthetic affectation of many
persons who have not enough of the artist in them to
work arduously and overcome technical difficulties, so
they live a life of self-indulgent sentimental artistic indo-
lence.^{CD Vol. 2}

Reflection Questions

*Is my spiritual life more of an illusion
than a reality? Am I more concerned
about making a favorable impression on
others than I am about being
truly spiritual?*

IF I PRAY that someone else may be, or do, something
which I am not, and don't intend to do, my praying is
paralyzed.^{DI}

Requires Discipline

PHYSICAL SLOTH WILL upset spiritual devotion quicker than anything else. If the devil cannot get at us by enticing to sin, he will get at us by sleeping-sickness spiritually—"No, you cannot possibly get up in the morning to pray, you are working hard all day and you cannot give that time to prayer. God does not expect it of you." Jesus says God does expect it of us. Penance means doing a hardship to the body for the sake of developing the spiritual life.ᔆᔆᴹ

Reflection Questions

Am I willing to give up physical comforts and convenience for spiritual well-being?

THE ILLUSTRATIONS OF prayer our Lord uses are on the line of importunity, a steady persistent, uninterrupted habit of prayer.ᴰᴵ

IF YOU TRY and settle down before God in prayer when you have been dwelling in unrealities, you will recognize instantly the condition of things. As soon as you get down to pray you remember a letter you ought to write, or something else that needs to be done, a thousand and one little impertinences come in and claim your attention. When we suspend our own activities and get down at the foot of the Cross and meditate there, God brings His thoughts to us by the Holy Spirit and interprets them to us.ᴹꜰᴸ

Reflection Questions

How often do I give in to the distractions that interrupt my prayers? What can I do to break this habit?

THE VERY POWERS of darkness are paralyzed by prayer. No wonder Satan tries to keep our minds fussy in active work "till we cannot think to pray."ᴿᵀᴿ

PRAYER IS NOT an emotion, not a sincere desire; prayer is the most stupendous effort of the will. "Let your requests be made known to God. And the peace of God, which will pass all understanding, will guard your hearts and minds through Christ Jesus." The power of the peace of God will enable you to steer your course in the mix-up of ordinary life.^{MFL}

Reflection Questions

How long has it been since I've had peace about what God is doing in my life? Why? Am I allowing God to do what He wants to in my life?

GET INTO THE habit of saying, "Speak, Lord," and life will become a romance. Every time circumstances press, say, "Speak, Lord," and make time to listen. Chastening is more than a means of discipline, it is meant to get me to the place of saying, "Speak, Lord."^{MUH}

PRAYER IS OFTEN a temptation to bank on a miracle of God instead of on a moral issue; that is, it is much easier to ask God to do my work than it is to do it myself. Until we are disciplined properly, we will always be inclined to bank on God's miracles and refuse to do the moral thing ourselves. It is our job, and it will never be done unless we do it.[SA]

Reflection Questions

What am I trying to get God to do that I should do myself? Restore a relationship? Resolve a problem at work? Choose my career? What will I take responsibility for today?

OH, WELL, I will pray and ask God to clean this thing up for me." God won't. We must do our own work. God will do more than we can do, but only in relationship to our spiritual growth.[PH]

68

WE TALK ABOUT the difficulty of living a holy life; yet we have the absolute simple ease provided by Almighty God for living a holy life because He paid so much to make it possible. Beware of placing the emphasis on what prayer costs us; it cost God everything to make it possible for us to pray.[IYA]

Reflection Questions

When was the last time I thought about the price Christ paid for me to have access to God? How might this thought change my attitude toward prayer?

IF ANYONE HAS a difficulty in getting through to God, it is never God who is to blame. We can get through to Him as soon as we want to, there is nothing simpler. The trouble is when we begin to sympathize with the thing that is proud and strong in independence of God.[PR]

ONE OF THE disciples said, "Lord, teach us to pray." The disciples were good men and well-versed in Jewish praying, yet when they came in contact with Jesus Christ, instead of realizing they could pray well, they came to the conclusion they did not know how to pray at all, and our Lord instructed them in the initial stages of prayer.

We become conscious not only of the power God has given us by His Spirit, but of our own utter infirmity. We hinder our life of devotion when we lose the distinction between these two. Reliance on the Holy Spirit for prayer is what Luke is bringing out in this verse. It is an unrealized point. We state it glibly, but Luke touches the thing we need to remember: the truth of our infirmity.[IYA]

Reflection Questions

Do I allow myself to get close enough to Jesus so that He can reveal to me my infirmities?

A Holy Occupation
Requires Faith

STATE DEFINITELY TO yourself the things that are confused; note the things that are not clear black and white. There are no problems at all over right and wrong. Human life is not made up of right and wrong, but of things which are not quite clear. Stand in faith that what Jesus said is true—Everyone who asks receives. If the friendship of God is shrouded and it looks as if He is not going to do anything, then remain mute. The real problems are very heavy. Remember, God has bigger issues at stake on the ground of redemption than the particular setting in which we ask.ᴾᴴ

Reflection Questions
Do I try to see the bigger issues of redemption when I pray or do I only see my own circumstances?

PRAYER IS THE supreme activity of all that is noblest in our personality and the essential nature of prayer is faith.ᴺᴷᵂ

OUR LORD, IN instructing the disciples in regard to prayer, presented them with three pictures (see Luke 11:1–13 and 18:1–8), and strangely puzzling pictures they are until we understand their meaning. They are the pictures of an unkind friend, an unnatural father, and an unjust judge. Like many of our Lord's answers, these pictures seem no answer at all at first; they seem evasions, but we find that in answering our inarticulate questions our Lord presents His answer to the reality discernible to conscience, and not to logic.^{CD Vol. 2}

Reflection Questions
What is the difference between the reality discernible to conscience and the reality discernible to logic?

GOD PUTS US in circumstances where He can answer the prayer of His Son and the prayer of the Holy Spirit.^{DI}

IF OUR FATHER knows what we need before we ask, why ask? The point of prayer is not in order to get answers from God; prayer is perfect and complete oneness with God. If we pray because we want answers, we will get huffed with God. The answers come every time, but not always in the way we expect, and our spiritual huff shows a refusal to identify ourselves with our Lord in prayer.ᴹᵁᴴ

Reflection Questions
How do I respond when God does not answer as I expect? Do I accept His answer willingly or grudgingly?

CHILDREN OF GOD never pray to be conscious that God answers prayer, because they are so restfully certain that God always does answer prayer.ᴹᵁᴴ

Requires Faith

OUR LORD SAYS that God the Father will give the Holy Spirit much more readily than we would give good gifts to our children, and the Holy Spirit not only brings us into the zone of God's influence but into intimate relationship with Him personally, so that by the slow discipline of prayer the choices of our free will become the preordinations of His Almighty order. God does not give faith in answer to prayer; He reveals Himself in answer to prayer, and faith is exercised spontaneously.[DI]

Reflection Questions
What have I learned about God today as
a result of my prayers?

GOD IS NOT meant to answer *our* prayers, He is answering the prayer of Jesus Christ in our lives. By our prayers we come to discern what God's mind is.[DI]

75

DO I EXPECT God to answer prayer? The first thing that will stagger faith in God is the false sentiment arising out of a sympathetic apprehension of the difficulties. Peter therefore was kept in prison, but prayer was made earnestly of the church unto God for him: the church prayed, and God did the impossible thing, and Peter was delivered. We have to pray with our eyes on God, not on the difficulties.GW

Reflection Questions
How will my prayer life be different if I
focus on God rather than on
my circumstances?

JOB'S CRY, "OH, that I knew where I might find Him," is the birth of evangelical prayer on the basis of redemption. The finding cannot be by reasoning or by religious faith; the only way to find God is through prayer.BFB

IN REGENERATION GOD works below the threshold of our consciousness; all we are conscious of is a sudden burst up into our conscious life, but as to when God begins to work no one can tell. This emphasizes the importance of intercessory prayer. A mother, a husband or a wife, or a Christian worker praying for another soul has a clear indication that God has answered their prayer; outwardly the one prayed for is just the same, there is no difference in his conduct but the prayer is answered. The work is unconscious as yet, but at any second it may burst forth into conscious life. We cannot calculate where God begins to work any more than we can say when it is going to become conscious; that is why we have to pray in reliance on the Holy Spirit.[BP]

Reflection Questions
*Even if I see no change,
I am going to pray indefinitely for
the conversion of . . .*

I THINK SOMETIMES we will be covered with shame when we meet the Lord Jesus and think how blind and ignorant we were when He brought people around us to pray for and instead of praying we tried to find out what was wrong. We have no business to try and find out what is wrong; our business is to pray so that when the awakening comes Jesus Christ will be the first they meet.^{OPG}

Reflection Questions

Do I concentrate more on what is wrong
with people than on praying that they
will be made right with God?

THE KNOWLEDGE OF where people are wrong is a hindrance to prayer, not an assistance. "I want to tell you of the difficulties so that you may pray intelligently." The more you know the less intelligently you pray because you forget to believe that God can alter the difficulties.^{GW 21}

IF I BELIEVE in God I pray on the ground of redemption and things happen; it is not reasonable, it is redemptive. Where reason says "There is a mountain, it is impossible," I do not argue and say "I believe God can remove it," I do not even see the mountain; I simply set my face toward the Lord God and make my prayer, and the mountain ceases to be.[HGM]

Reflection Questions

When I pray, do I concentrate more on the "mountain" I want removed or on God, who can remove it?

THE SECRET OF our inefficiency for God is that we do not believe what He tells us about prayer. Prayer is not relational but redemptive. Little books of prayer are full of "buts." The New Testament says that God will answer prayer every time. The point is not—"will you believe?" but "will I, who know Jesus Christ, believe on your behalf?"[RTR]

YOU SAY, "BUT I asked God to turn my life into a garden of the Lord, and there came the ploughshare of sorrow, and instead of a garden I have been given a wilderness." God never gives a wrong answer. The garden of your natural life had to be turned into ploughed soil before God could turn it into a garden of the Lord. He will put the seed in now. Let God's seasons come over your soul, and before long your life will be a garden of the Lord.SSM

Reflection Questions

When my life is as barren as a recently plowed field, do I let the enemy come along and plant weeds before God plants His crop?

BY MEANS OF intercession we understand more and more the way God solves the problems produced in our minds by the conflict of actual facts and our real faith in God.NKW

YOU SAY, "BUT I don't feel that God is my Father." Jesus said, "Say it." Say "Our Father," and you will suddenly discover that He is. The safeguard against moral imprisonment is prayer. Don't pray according to your moods, but resolutely launch out on God, say "Our Father," and before you know where you are, you are in a larger room.ᴾᴴ

Reflection Questions
How does my own moodiness affect
my prayer life?

TO BE SO much in contact with God that you never need to ask Him to show you His will is to be nearing the final stage of your discipline in the life of faith. When you are rightly related to God, it is a life of freedom and liberty and delight; you are God's will, and all your commonsense decisions are His will for you.ᴹᵁᴴ

MEDITATION MEANS GETTING to the middle of a thing. The majority of us attend only to the "muddle" of things, consequently we get spiritual indigestion, the counterpart of physical indigestion, a desperately gloomy state of affairs. We cannot see anything rightly, and all we do see is stars. "Faith is . . . the evidence of things not seen." Suppose Jesus suddenly lifted the veil from our eyes and let us see angels ministering to us, His own Presence with us, the Holy Spirit in us, and the Father around us, how amazed we should be! We have lived in the muddle of things instead of in the middle of things. Faith gets us into the middle, which is God and God's purpose. Elisha prayed for his servant, "Lord, I pray, open his eyes that he may see"; and when his eyes were opened he saw the hosts of God and nothing else.MFL

Reflection Questions

*Do I see God or my enemies
when I pray?*

A Holy Occupation
Requires Honesty

ASK MEANS BEG. Some people are poor enough to be interested in their poverty, and some of us are like that spiritually. We will never receive if we ask out of our lust rather than out of our poverty. A pauper who asks from no other reason than the abject panging condition of his poverty is not ashamed to beg. Blessed are the poor in spirit.MUH

Reflection Questions
What would be different about my life
and prayers if I were truly
"poor in spirit"?

IT IS RARELY the big compellings of God that get hold of us in our prayers; instead we tell God what He should do. We tell Him that men are being lost and that He ought to save them. This is a terrific charge against God; it means that He might be asleep. Prayer with us often becomes merely a way of patronizing God.PR

NOTHING IS MORE difficult than asking. We long and desire and crave and suffer, but not until we are at the extreme limit will we ask. A sense of unreality makes us ask. We cannot bring ourselves up against spiritual reality when we like—all at once the staggering realization dawns that we are destitute of the Holy Spirit, ignorant of all that the Lord Jesus stands for. The first result of being brought up against reality is this realization of poverty, of the lack of wisdom, lack of the Holy Spirit, lack of power, lack of a grip of God. "If any of you lacks wisdom, let him ask of God."OBH

Reflection Questions
Am I willing to pray for wisdom and to
see myself as God sees me?

TO BE CONSCIOUSLY desirous of anything but that one thing is to be off the main track. The Holy Spirit is transparent honesty.HGM

KNOCK AND IT will be opened to you. . . . Draw near to God. Knock—the door is closed, and you suffer from palpitation as you knock. "Cleanse your hands"—knock a bit louder, you begin to find you are dirty. "Purify your heart"—this is more personal still, you are desperately in earnest now—you will do anything. "Lament"—have you ever lamented before God at the state of your inner life? There is no strand of self-pity left, but a heartbreaking affliction of amazement to find you are the kind of person that you are. "Humble yourself"—it is a humbling business to knock at God's door—you have to knock with the crucified thief. "To him who knocks, it will be opened."ᴹᵁᴴ

Reflection Questions
What do my prayers reveal about the kind of person I am?

Requires Honesty

HOW MANY OF us pray simply in order to feel the presence and blessing of God upon us, and mistake that for the answer? Such prayer is not transaction with God at all; it is in its final analysis an indulgence of the finer sensibilities. This idea of prayer gives rise to the thought of the present day that prayer is merely a reflex action on the life which quietens it, whereas New Testament praying is getting hold of a personal God through the opening up of a channel whereby God can deal directly with those for whom we pray. Such prayer humbles the soul always, and gives the life the benediction of being rightly related to God.ᴳᵂ

Reflection Questions

Are my prayers more of a selfish indulgence than an honest attempt to be rightly related to God?

OUR LORD SAYS, "Ask," and we will always find that we do not ask when we talk about it. "I'll pray about it"—but we won't. To say we will pray about a thing often means we are determined not to think about it. Contact with Jesus Christ made the disciples realize that they were paupers, and they said, "Lord, teach us to pray."PR

Reflection Questions

The disciples, after being around Jesus, wanted to learn to pray. If I do not yet see the need to pray, what does that say about my closeness to Jesus?

BE YOURSELF EXACTLY before God, and present your problems, the things you know you have come to your wits' end about. Ask what you will, and Jesus Christ says your prayers will be answered. We can always tell whether our will is in what we ask by the way we live when we are not praying.IYA

THERE IS A difference between God's order and God's permissive will. We say that God will see us through if we trust Him—"I prayed for my boy, and he was spared in answer to my prayer." Does that mean that the man who was killed was not prayed for, or that prayers for him were not answered? It is wrong to say that in the one case the man was delivered by prayer but not in the other. It is a misunderstanding of what Jesus Christ reveals.^{SHH}

Reflection Questions

How am I deceiving myself if I believe that whenever I get what I want it is an answer to prayer?

THE NEXT BEST thing to do if you are not spiritually real, is to ask God for the Holy Spirit on the word of Jesus Christ. . . . The Holy Spirit is the One who makes real in you all that Jesus did for you.^{MUH}

YOU VERY EARNESTLY and solemnly tax your resources to be a praying person; people call at your house but cannot see you because it is your time for prayer. You perhaps have not noticed before that you always take care to tell those to whom it matters how early you rise in the morning to pray, how many all nights of prayer you spend; you have great zealousness in proclaiming your protracted meetings. This is all pious play-acting. Jesus says, "Don't do it."^{CD Vol. 2}

Reflection Questions

*How much of my praying is dishonest
in that it is done to impress
other people?*

THE PRAYER OF the saints is never self-important, but always God-important.^{DI}

Requires Honesty

AM I MAKING the Holy Spirit's work difficult by being indefinite or by trying to do His work for Him? I must do the human side of intercession, and the human side is the circumstances I am in and the people I am in contact with. I have to keep my conscious life as a shrine of the Holy Spirit. Then as I bring the people before God, the Holy Spirit makes intercession for them.ᴹᵁᴴ

Reflection Questions
Of the things I strive to accomplish, what should I leave in God's hands?

QUIT PRAYING ABOUT yourself and be spent for others as the bondslave of Jesus. That is the meaning of being made broken bread and poured out wine in reality.ᴹᵁᴴ

IF WE HAVE not caught the meaning of the tremendous moral aspect of the Atonement it is because we have never prayed this prayer, "Search me, O God." Are we sincere enough to ask God to search us, and sincere enough to abide by what His searching reveals?[SHL]

Reflection Questions

Which of my convictions have more to do with my own personal preferences than with God's revelation?

WE DO NOT get insight by struggling, but by going to God in prayer. Most of us are wise in our own opinions, we have emotions of our own which we want to see through. There is nothing to be valued more highly than to have people praying for us; God links up His power in answer to their prayers.[BFB]

Requires Honesty

THE MAN WHO prays ceases to be a fool, while the man who refuses to pray nourishes a blind life without his own brain and he will find no way out that road. Job cries out that prayer is the only way out in all these matters.[BFB]

Reflection Questions

Is prayer a road I regularly travel or one that I use only when I can find no easier route?

THE POSITION WE are apt to give to prayer is too consciously an attainment of communion, and thus it is presented out of all proportion, so that in times of spiritual declension we are inclined to place the need of prayer instead of penitent approach to God in the forefront.[CD Vol. 2]

IF WE ARE not heedful of the way the Spirit of God works in us, we will become spiritual hypocrites. We see where other folks are failing, and we turn our discernment into the gibe of criticism instead of into intercession on their behalf. The revelation is made to us not through the acuteness of our minds, but by the direct penetration of the Spirit of God. And if we are not heedful of the source of the revelation, we will become criticizing centers and forget that God says, "ask, and I will give him life who commits sin not leading to death." Take care lest you play the hypocrite by spending all your time trying to get others right before you worship God yourself.[MUH]

Reflection Questions
Of whom am I the most critical?
How can I pray for that person honestly and unselfishly?

A Holy Occupation
Requires Intimacy

THE WAY WE react during the day will either hinder or help our praying. If we allow a state of reaction not born of a simple relationship to Jesus Christ, we shall have so much wilderness waste to get through before we can come to God, mists and shadows which come between our conscious life and the interceding Holy Spirit. The Holy Spirit is there all the time, but we have lost sight of Him by allowing things that have not sprung from our simple relationship to Jesus Christ. Anything that is so continually with us, even our religious life itself, that we never really pray in the Holy Spirit, may be a hindrance. The only one who prays in the Holy Spirit is the child, the child-spirit in us, the simple spirit of utter confidence in God.[IYA]

Reflection Questions

_Did my reaction to circumstances
yesterday help or hinder my prayer life?
What will I do differently today?_

THE DEVOTION OF the saint is to "fill up in my flesh what is lacking in the afflictions of Christ, for the sake of His body." How can we fill up the sufferings that remain? First John 5:16 is an indication of one way—that of intercession. Remember, no one has time to pray; we have to take time from other things that are valuable in order to understand how necessary prayer is. The things that act like thorns and stings in our personal lives will go away instantly we pray; we won't feel the smart any more, because we have God's point of view about them. Prayer means that we get into union with God's view of other people. Our devotion as saints is to identify ourselves with God's interests in other lives. God pays no attention to our personal affinities; He expects us to identify ourselves with His interests in others.[PR]

Reflection Questions
What person do I need to see in the same way as God sees him or her?

THINK OF THE unfathomable bliss of the revelation that we shall perceive our Father solving our problems, and shall understand Him; it is the reward of the joyous time of prayer. In all the temptations that contend in our hearts, and amid the things that meet us in the providence of God which seem to involve a contradiction of His fatherhood, the secret place convinces us that He is our Father and that He is righteousness and love, and we remain not only unshaken but we receive our reward with an intimacy that is unspeakable and full of glory.CD Vol. 2

Reflection Questions
What more do I expect from God than the
joy of His presence when I pray?

IF WE ARE abiding in Jesus and His words are abiding in us, God will answer our prayers.OBH

IT IS AN insult to sink before God and say, "Your will be done" when there has been no intercession. That is the prayer of impertinent unbelief—there is no use in praying, God does whatever He chooses. The saying of "Your will be done" is born of the most intimate relationship to God whereby I talk to Him freely. There is in this prayer of Abraham a distinction between the begging which knows no limit and the prayer which is conscious that there are limits set by the holy character of God. Repetition in intercessory importunity is not bargaining, but the joyous insistence of prayer. NKW

Reflection Questions

When I pray "Your will be done" am I doing so only because it is easier than finding out what the will of God is?

THE REASON FOR prayer is intimacy of relation with our Father. CD Vol. 2

ONE OF THE most subtle burdens God ever puts on us as saints is this burden of discernment concerning other souls. He reveals things in order that we may take the burden of these souls before Him and form the mind of Christ about them. It is not that we bring God into touch with our minds, but that we rouse ourselves until God is able to convey His mind to us about the one for whom we intercede.ᴹᵁᴴ

Reflection Questions

What might God be telling me about a particular person for whom I've been praying?

PRAYER IN THE Son of God as Son of Man is amazingly significant. If prayer is the highest reach of communion possible between Almighty God and the Son of Man, what part ought prayer to play in our lives?ᴾᴿ

Requires Intimacy

OUR LORD IN His teaching regarding prayer never once referred to unanswered prayer; He said God always answers prayer. If our prayers are in the name of Jesus, that is, in accordance with His nature, the answers will not be in accordance with our nature, but with His. We are apt to forget this, and to say without thinking that God does not always answer prayer. He does every time, and when we are in close communion with Him, we realize that we have not been misled.[IYA]

Reflection Questions
Am I close enough to God to recognize
His answers to prayer?

WHENEVER WE STOP short in prayer and say—"Well, I don't know; perhaps it is not God's will," there is still another stage to go. We are not so intimately acquainted with God as Jesus was, and as He wants us to be.[MUH]

Is JESUS CHRIST seeing the result of the labor of His soul in us? He cannot unless we are so identified with Him that we are roused up to get His view about the people for whom we pray. May we learn to intercede so whole-heartedly that Jesus Christ will be abundantly satisfied with us as intercessors.ᴹᵁᴴ

Reflection Questions

Do I take prayer as seriously as Jesus does? How would I pray differently if Jesus were kneeling next to me?

WHEN IN DOUBT physically, dare; when in moral doubt, stop; when in spiritual doubt, pray; and when in personal doubt, be guided by your life with God. Base all on God, and slowly and surely the actual life will be educated along the particular line of your relationship to Him.ˢᴴᴴ

A WONDERFUL THING about God's silence is that the contagion of His stillness gets into you and you become perfectly confident—"I know God has heard me." His silence is the proof that He has. As long as you have the idea that God will bless you in answer to prayer, He will do it, but He will never give you the grace of silence. If Jesus Christ is bringing you into the understanding that prayer is for the glorifying of His Father, He will give you the first sign of His intimacy—silence.MUH

Reflection Questions
Am I close enough to God to feel secure
even when He is silent?

OUR LORD'S VIEW of prayer is that it represents the highest reach possible to a man or woman when rightly related to God, perfectly obedient in every particular, and in perfect communion with Him.PR

INTERCESSION LEAVES YOU neither time nor inclination to pray for your own "sad sweet self." The thought of yourself is not kept out because it is not there to keep out; you are completely and entirely identified with God's interest in other lives.ʀᴛʀ

Reflection Questions
Is there too much of me and too little of others in my prayers?

I DO NOT say to you that I shall pray the Father for you; for the Father Himself loves you. Have you reached such an intimacy with God that the Lord Jesus Christ's life of prayer is the only explanation of your life of prayer? Has our Lord's vicarious life become your vital life? "In that day" you will be so identified with Jesus that there will be no distinction.ᴍᴜʜ

A Holy Occupation
Requires Obedience

IN OUR LORD'S life there was no divorce between the ideal and the real; He never gave Himself continually to prayer. Beware of the tendency that makes you wish that God would pretend you are someone special. It is a childish make-believe, standing on spiritual tiptoe to look as big as God—others can do this and that, but I must give myself to prayer. The great secret of the obedient life of faith is that the real conditions of bodily life are transfigured by real communion with God.NKW

Reflection Questions

Is my prayer life confined to a certain time and place? If so, how can I broaden it to make it a part of everything I do?

THE REASON FOR intercession is not that God answers prayer, but that God tells us to pray.DI

Requires Obedience

JESUS DID NOT say, "Go into the field," He said, "therefore pray the Lord of the harvest . . ." That does not so much mean that the harvest is the world, it means that there are innumerable people who have reached crises in their lives and are "already white for harvest." We find them everywhere, not only in foreign countries, but in the houses next door to us. The way we discern is not by intellect, not by suggestions, but by prayer.[IYA]

Reflection Questions

In what areas do I rely more on my own common sense than on prayer?

WE DISCERN SPIRITUAL truth not by intellectual curiosity or research, but by entreating the favor of the Lord, that is, by prayer and by no other way, not even by obedience, because obedience is apt to have an idea of merit.[HGM]

INSTEAD OF PRAYING to the Lord of the harvest to send out laborers we pray—"O Lord, keep my body right; see after this matter and that for me." Our prayers are taken up with our concerns, our own needs, and only once in a while do we pray for what He tells us to.[SSY]

Reflection Questions
What are the things God wants me to pray for?

TO BE SPIRITUAL by effort is a sure sign of a false relationship to God; to be obedient by effort in the initial stages is a sure sign that we are determined to obey God at all costs.[MFL]

WHEN WE COME to the repleteness of "yes," the moral miracle God works in us is that we ask only what is exactly in accordance with God's nature, and the repleteness begins, the fullness and satisfaction of the "Everlasting Yes." That does not mean that God will give us everything we ask for, but that God can do with us now exactly what He likes. We have no business to tell God we cannot stand any more; God ought to be at liberty to do with us what He chooses, as He did with His own Son. Then whatever happens our lives will be full of joy.PH

Reflection Questions
Do I give God the same freedom to do
with me as He gives me to do with Him?

GOD EXPECTS US to be intercessors, not dogmatic fault-finders, but vicarious intercessors, until other lives come up to the same standard.HG

IT IS ABSURD to imagine anyone trying to think how they will live before they are born, yet it is this absurdity which the intellect tries to perform in connection with prayer. If the dominion of intellectual explanation is the characteristic of a naturally cultured life, dominion by obedience is the characteristic of the spiritually disciplined life. Intellectual expression in life is the effect of a naturally educated life, but is not the cause of the life; and the Christian experience of prayer is not its own cause, but the effect of the life of God in me.^{CD Vol. 2}

Reflection Questions
If my life were the only evidence that
Christ is alive, would anyone
be convinced?

SEE THAT YOU do not use the trick of prayer to cover up what you know you ought to do.^{DI}

ASK YOURSELF HOW much time you have taken up asking God that you may not do the things you do. He will never answer; you have simply not to do them. Every time God speaks, there is something we must obey. We should do well to revise what we pray about. Some of the things we pray about are as absurd as if we prayed, "O Lord, take me out of this room," and then refused to go.^{MFL}

Reflection Questions

What temptation do I continually give in to? Instead of praying "Give me the strength to resist" (which God has already done), what might happen if I were to pray "Give me the will to use the strength You have made available"?

HE DOES NOT say, "Do good to those who despitefully use you." He says, "Pray for those who despitefully use you."^{SSM}

AS YOU, FATHER, *are in Me, and I in You; that they also may be one in Us.* Prayer is not getting things from God. That is a most initial stage; prayer is getting into perfect communion with God: I tell Him what I know He knows in order that I may get to know it as He does.[SSM]

*R*eflection *Q*uestions

Which do I obey more often, the urges of my body or the nudges of God's Spirit?

MUCH OF THE misery in our Christian life comes not because the devil tackles us, but because we have never understood the simple laws of our makeup. We have to treat the body as the servant of Jesus Christ; when the body says, "Sit" and He says, "Go," go! When the body says "Eat," and He says, "Fast," fast! When the body says "Yawn," and He says, "Pray," pray![BE]

Requires Obedience

WHEN GOD PUTS a weight on you for intercession for souls don't shirk it by talking to them. It is much easier to talk to them than to talk to God about them—much easier to talk to them than to take it before God and let the weight crush the life out of you until gradually and patiently God lifts the life out of the mire. That is where very few of us go.ᴳᵂ

Reflection Questions
For whom would God have me
intercede today?

ARE WE LEARNING to bring ourselves into such obedience that our every thought and imagination is brought into captivity to the Lord Jesus Christ? Remember, your intercessions can never be mine, and my intercessions can never be yours, but without both of them someone will be impoverished. Let us remember the depth and height and solemnity of our calling as saints.ᴵᵞᴬ

IF YOU HAVE incurred a debt and not paid it, nor cared about paying it, or have spoken in the wrong mood to another, or been vindictive—these and similar things produce a wrong temper of soul and you cannot pray in secret. It is no use trying to pray until you do what the Lord says. The one thing that keeps us from doing it is pride, and pride has never yet prayed in the history of mankind.^{CD Vol. 2}

*R*eflection *Q*uestions
*In what area of my life does pride
hinder obedience?*

OUR PRAYERS FOR God's help are often nothing but incarnate laziness, and God has to say, "Speak no more to Me of this matter. Get up!"^{MFL}

Requires Obedience

YOU HAVE A wrong attitude of mind towards another, and the Spirit of God tells you to put it right between yourself and that one and you say—No, I will put it right between myself and God. You cannot do it; it is impossible. Instead of deliberately obeying God, irrespective of what it costs, we use the trick of prayer to cover our own cowardice.^{NKW}

Reflection Questions

Which of my prayers are no more than a coverup of my cowardliness?

DON'T PUT PRAYER and obedience in the place of the Cross of Christ—"Because I have obeyed, Christ will do this or that." He won't. The only way we are saved and sanctified is by the free grace of God.^{RTR}

PRAY FOR YOUR friends, and God will turn your captivity also. The emancipation comes as you intercede for them; it is not a mere reaction, it is the way God works. It is not a question of getting time for Bible study, but of spontaneous intercession as we go about out daily calling. We shall see emancipation come all along, not because we understand the problems, but because we recognize that God has chosen the way of intercession to perform His moral miracles in lives. Then get to work and pray, and God will get His chance with other lives; you do not even need to speak to them. God has based the Christian life on redemption, and as we pray on this basis God's honor is at stake to answer prayer.[BFB]

Reflection Questions

Do I feel imprisoned by my own flesh? How might that change if I were to concentrate on praying that others in bondage would be freed?

A Holy Occupation
Requires Patience

GOD DOES NOT exist to answer our prayers, but by our prayers we come to discern the mind of God, and that is declared in John 17, "That they may be one, as we are." Am I as close to Jesus as that? God will not leave me alone until I am. God has one prayer He must answer, and that is the prayer of Jesus Christ. It does not matter how imperfect or immature a disciple may be, if he will hand in, that prayer will be answered.[IYA]

Reflection Questions
Do all my prayers have a single purpose: "that we may be one"?

SOME PRAYERS ARE so big, and God has such a surprising answer for us, that He keeps us waiting for the manifestation.[PH]

Requires Patience

THE EFFECT PRAYER has on ourselves is the building up of our character in the understanding of God; that is why we need patience in prayer. We cannot "by one wild bound, clear the numberless ascensions of starry stairs." How impatient we are in dealing with other people! Our actions imply that we think God is asleep, until God brings us to the place where we finally see others from His viewpoint.[DI]

Reflection Questions

If God, Who is perfect, can be patient with me even though I am imperfect, why can't I be patient with Him?

IT IS ONE thing to cry to God and another thing to hear Him answer. We don't give God time to answer. We come in a great fuss and panic, but when all that is taken out of our hearts and we are silent before God, the quiet certainty comes—"I know God has heard me."[HG]

MEN ALWAYS OUGHT *to pray, and not lose heart.* Jesus also taught the disciples the prayer of patience. If you are right with God and God delays the answer to your prayer, don't misjudge Him. Don't think of Him as an unkind friend, or an unnatural father, or an unjust judge, but keep at it. Your prayer will certainly be answered, for "everyone who asks receives." Pray and do not cave in. Your heavenly Father will explain it all one day. He cannot just yet because He is developing your character.^{SSM}

Reflection Questions
Which of my prayers seem to have
no satisfying answer?

GOD ALWAYS ANSWERS the stumbling questions which arise out of personal problems. We bristle with interrogation points, but we don't wait for the answer because we do not intend to listen to it.^{RTR}

Requires Patience

WE ASK AMISS when we ask simply with the determination to outdo the patience of God until He gives us permission to do what we want to do. Such asking is mere sentimental unreality. And we ask amiss when we ask things from life and not from God; asking from the desire for self-realization is in direct opposition to Christ's desire for us. The more we realize ourselves the less we will rely on God. Are we asking things of God or of life?OBH

Reflection Questions

Am I satisfied with what God gives me or do I want what the world has to give as well? When I pray am I truly trying to find out who God is, or am I trying to find out who I am?

PRAY BECAUSE YOU have a Father, not because it quietens you, and give Him time to answer.SSM

TAKE TIME. REMEMBER we have all the time there is. The majority of us waste time and want to encroach on eternity. "Oh well, I think about these things when I have time." The only time you will have is the day after you are dead, and that will be eternity. An hour, or half an hour, of daily attention to, and meditation on, our own spiritual life is the secret of progress.MFL

Reflection Questions

What do I do every day that is more important than spending time with God?

HOW STEADILY ALL through the Old and New Testament God calls us to stand on the watch and wait for His indications, and how often God's answers to our prayers have been squandered because we do not watch and wait.IYA

Requires Patience

THE ONLY WAY to keep right is to watch and pray. Prayer on any other basis than that on which it is placed in the New Testament is stupid, and the basis of prayer is not human earnestness, not human need, not the human will, it is redemption, and its living center is a personal Holy Spirit.[IYA]

Reflection Questions
How often do I whine and cry instead of watch and pray?

THE MEANING OF waiting in both the Old and New Testament is "standing under," actively enduring. It is not standing with folded arms doing nothing; it is not saying, "In God's good time it will come to pass"—that often means in my abominably lazy time I let God work. Waiting means standing under, in active strength, enduring till the answer comes.[IYA]

WHEN THE SOUL is perplexed—and it certainly will be if we are going on with God, because we are a mark for Satan—and the sudden onslaught comes, as it did in the life of Job, we cry, "Heal me because of my pain," but there is no answer. Then we cry, "Heal me, not because I am in pain, but because my soul is perplexed; I cannot see any way out of it or why this thing should be"; still no answer; then at last we cry, "Heal me, O Lord, not because of my pain, nor because my soul is sick, but for your mercy's sake." Then we have the answer, "The Lord has heard my supplication."[BP]

Reflection Questions

What is perplexing me today? What is the proper way to pray about it?

WATCH FOR GOD'S answer to your prayers, and not only watch, but wait.[IYA]

A Holy Occupation

Requires Power

MEDITATION MEANS GETTING to the middle of a thing; not being like a pebble in a brook and letting the water of thought go over us; that is reverie, not meditation. Meditation is an intense spiritual activity. It means bringing every bit of the mind into harness and concentrating its powers; it includes both deliberation and reflection. Deliberation means being able to weigh well what we think, conscious all the time that we are deliberating and meditating. "My heart consulted in me" is exactly the meaning of meditation.[BP]

Reflection Questions
How much of my praying is true meditation and how much is simple reverie?

PRAYER IMPARTS THE power to walk and not faint, and the lasting remembrance of our lives is of the Lord, not of us.[IYA]

Requires Power

IN WORK FOR God never look at flesh and blood causes; meet every arrangement for the day in the power of the Holy Ghost. It makes no difference what your work is, or what your circumstances are; if you are praying in the Holy Ghost, He will produce an atmosphere round about you, and all these things will redound to the glory of God.[IYA]

Reflection Questions
In my work for God, what are the areas
in which I rely too much on my own
strength and too little on God's?

PRAYING IN THE Holy Spirit means the power given to us by God to maintain a simple relationship to Jesus Christ, and it is most difficult to realize this simple relationship in the matter of prayer.[IYA]

JESUS SAID THAT God will recognize our prayers. What a challenge! Had Jesus any right to say it? Have we faced it for one moment? Is it possible that the Lord Jesus Christ means that by His resurrection power, by His Ascension power, by the power of the Sent-down Holy Spirit, He can lift us into such a relationship with God that we are at one with the perfect, sovereign will of God by our free choice as Jesus was? Does He mean what He says?[IYA]

Reflection Questions

If I were taking seriously Jesus' statement that my will could be aligned with the will of the sovereign God, how might my life be different?

THE MEANING OF prayer is that I bring power to bear upon another soul that is weak enough to yield and strong enough to resist; hence the need for strenuous intercessory prayer.[DI]

128

Requires Power

PRAYER IS NOT always a time of triumph; there are not only times of taking strongholds by storm, but times when spiritual darkness falls, when the great powers in the heavenlies are at work, when no one understands the wiles of Satan but God; at such times we have to stand steadily shoulder-to-shoulder for God. How often the Spirit of God emphasizes the "together-ness" of the saints.GW

Reflection Questions
Do I contribute more to the unity or disunity of believers?

THE HOLY SPIRIT has special prayers in every individual saint which bring him or her at times under the powerful searching of God. This searching of the heart is bewildering at first, but we are soon comforted by the realization that God is searching our hearts not for the convicting of sin, but to find out what is the mind of the Spirit.CD Vol. 2

PRAYER DOES NOT fit us for the greater works; prayer is the greater work. We think of prayer as a common-sense exercise of our higher powers in order to prepare us for God's work. In the teaching of Jesus Christ, prayer is the working of the miracle of redemption in me which produces the miracle of redemption in others by the power of God.ᴹᵁᴴ

Reflection Questions

Do I consider prayer a means to an end or an end in itself? Which should it be?

WE CAN CHOKE God's word with a yawn; we can hinder the time that should be spent with God by remembering we have other things to do. "I haven't time." Of course you have not time! Take time, strangle some other interests and make time to realize that the center of power in your life is the Lord Jesus Christ and His Atonement.ᴼᴮᴴ

O LORD, TO You do I come that I might find grace to praise and worship You aright. Lord, shine the light of Your face on us; send power and majestic grace. O Lord, how good it is for me to know You; how essentially necessary it is for me to draw nigh to You. How can I falter when You are my Life! Lord, our God, the Father of our Lord Jesus Christ, of Whom Jesus is the very image, I look to You and make my prayer. Bless me this hour with Your presence and nearness, for I do trust You and hope only in You.[IYA]

Reflection Questions
Can I honestly say that I hope only in God?

PRAYER IS THE outcome of our apprehension of the nature of God, the means whereby we assimilate more and more of His mind, and the means whereby He unveils His purposes to us.[SSY]

O LORD, MY Lord, I come to You this morning with a sense of spiritual failure. Cleanse me by Your grace and restore me to the heavenly places in Christ Jesus. O that the sweet kindness of Jesus were more and more manifest in me. O Lord, the range of Your power, the touch of Your grace, the breathing of Your Spirit, how I long for these to bring me face to face with You; Lord, by Your grace cause me to appear before You.[IYA]

Reflection Questions

What habit do I have that keeps the sweet kindness of Jesus from being manifested in my life? What am I going to do today to get rid of it?

WHAT HAPPENS WHEN saints pray is that the power of the almighty is brought to bear on the one for whom they are praying.[DI]

WHEN WE COME up against things in life, are we going to cave in and say we cannot understand them? We understand them by intercession, and by our intercession God does things He does not show us just now, although He reveals more and more of His character to us. He is working out His new creations in the world through His wonderful redemption and our intercession all the time, and we have to be sagacious, not impudent.[IYA]

Reflection Questions
What forces have I given in to rather than put into God's hands by way of intercession?

PRAYER MEANS THAT I come in contact with an Almighty Christ, and almighty results happen along the lines He laid down.[DI]

HOW BEAUTIFUL THIS undisturbed morning hour is with God! O Lord, this day my soul would stay upon You as Creator of the world, and upon our Lord Jesus Christ as Creator of His life in me. Oh for the power of Your Spirit to adore You in fuller measure! "What shall I give to the Lord for all His benefits toward me? I will take up the cup of salvation." Can I think of anything so gracious and complete in surrender and devotion and gratitude as to take from You? O Lord, I would that I had a livelier sense of You and of Your bounties continually with me. O Lord, this day may Your beauty and grace and soothing peace be in and upon me, and may no wind or weather or anxiety ever touch Your beauty and Your peace in my life or in this place.[IYA]

Reflection Questions

What do I allow into my life that destroys the beauty Jesus puts there?

A Holy Occupation
Requires Purpose

PRAYER ALTERS A man on the inside, alters his mind and his attitude to things. The point of praying is not that we get things from God, but that we learn by prayer to detect the difference between God's order and God's permissive will. God's order is—no pain, no sickness, no devil, no war, no sin; His permissive will is all these things. What a man needs to do is to get hold of God's order in the kingdom on the inside, and then he will begin to see how to handle the riddle of the universe on the outside.SHH

Reflection Questions

What might happen if I spent more time allowing God to change me and less time trying to change my circumstances?

GOD HAS SO constituted things that prayer on the basis of redemption alters the way a man looks at things.OBH

Requires Purpose

INTERCESSORY PRAYER IS part of the sovereign purpose of God. If there were no saints praying for us, our lives would be infinitely worse than they are; consequently the responsibility of those who never intercede and who are withholding blessing from our lives is truly appalling. The subject of intercessory prayer is weakened by the neglect of the idea with which we ought to start. We take for granted that prayer is preparation for work, whereas prayer is the work; and we scarcely believe what the Bible reveals—That God's chosen way of working is through intercessory prayer. We lean unto our own understanding, or we bank on service and do away with prayer. Consequently, by succeeding in the external we fail in the eternal, because in the eternal we succeed only by prevailing prayer. CD Vol. 2

Reflection Questions
From whom am I withholding God's
blessing by failing to pray for them?

AGREEMENT MUST NOT be taken to mean a prede-termination to storm God's fort doggedly till He yields. It is far from right to agree beforehand over what we want, and then go to God and wait, not until He gives us His mind about the matter, but until we extort from Him permission to do what we had made up our minds to do before we prayed; we should rather agree to ask God to convey His mind and meaning to us in regard to the matter. Agreement is not a public presentation of persistent begging which knows no limit, but a prayer which is conscious that it is limited through the moral nature of the Holy Spirit. It is really "symphonizing" on earth with our Father who is in heaven.CD Vol. 2

Reflection Questions

Do I listen to God singing the melody and then sing in harmony with Him or do I sing my own melody and urge Him to harmonize with me?

BEWARE OF HAVING plans in your petitions before God; they are the most fruitful source of misgiving. If you pray along the line of your plans, misgivings are sure to come. And if the misgivings are not heeded you will pervert God's purpose in the very thing which was begun at His bidding. God begins a work by the inspiration of the Holy Spirit for His own needs entirely, and we get caught up into His purpose for that thing. Then we begin to introduce our own plans—"I want this to produce that," and we storm the throne of God along that line. When God does not do it, we say, "That must be the devil." Beware of making God an item, even the principal item, in your program. God's ways are curiously abrupt with programs. He seems to delight in breaking them up.^{OPG}

Reflection Questions
Am I trying to build something for God
that He doesn't need or want?

OUR UNDERSTANDING OF God is the answer to prayer; getting things from God is God's indulgence of us. When God stops giving us things, He brings us into the place where we can begin to understand Him. As long as we get from God everything we ask for, we never get to know Him, we look upon Him as a blessing-machine that has nothing to do with God's character or with our characters.[IYA]

Reflection Questions

How much am I like a spoiled child who expects to get everything I want from God, my Father?

IT IS NOT sufficient for us to say, "Oh yes, God is love." We have to know He is love; we have to struggle through until we do see He is love and justice, then our prayer is answered.[IYA]

Requires Purpose

IT IS OF no use to pray for the old days; stand square where you are and make the present better than any past has been. Let people do what they like with your truth, but never explain it. Jesus never explained anything; we are always explaining, and we get into tangles by not leaving things alone. We need to pray St. Augustine's prayer, "O Lord, deliver me from this lust of always vindicating myself."SSM

Reflection Questions

If I am truly confident that I am acting in God's will, why do I bother trying to defend myself?

THE WHOLE IDEA of the prayers of the saints is that God's holiness, God's purpose, and God's wise ways may be brought about irrespective of who comes or goes.HGM

PRAYER IS NOT to be used as the privilege of a spoiled child seeking ideal conditions in which to indulge spiritual propensities without restraint. The purpose of prayer is the maintenance of fitness in an ideal relationship with God amid conditions which ought not to be merely ideal but real. Circumstances are not to be idealized, but to be realized, while by prayer we lay hold on God and He unites us into His consciousness.CD Vol. 2

Reflection Questions

*Do I pray so that I will be spiritually fit
or do I throw spiritual fits when I pray?*

PRAYER IS THE vital breath of Christians; not the thing that makes us alive, but the evidence that we are alive.DI

IT IS NOT so true that prayer changes things as that prayer changes me, and then I change things; consequently we must not ask God to do what He has created us to do. For instance, Jesus Christ is not a social reformer; He came to alter us first, and if there is any social reform to be done on earth, we must do it.[IYA]

Reflection Questions

How can I achieve the proper balance between praying for something to be done and working to get it done?

PRAYER IS NOT meant to develop us naturally, it is meant to give the life of the Son of God in us a chance to develop that the natural order may be transfigured into the spiritual.[PH]

JESUS PRAYED, "THAT they may be one, as We are"; and when Paul urges us to put on the new man, he is urging on the most practical line that we put on in our actual life the habits that are in perfect accordance with this oneness with God, and that we do it all the time. Then there will come the simple satisfaction of knowing that God is answering the prayer of Jesus Christ. If you want to know what God is after in your life, read John 17. How close to God is Jesus Christ? "I and My Father are One." That is what He asks for us, and the Father will not leave us alone until the prayer is answered. Are we hindering the power of God in our lives? Then never let us blame God.^{PR}

*R*eflection *Q*uestions

In what ways do I hinder unity among believers? In what ways do I hinder the power of God in my life?

A Holy Occupation

Requires Silence

THINK OF THOSE days of absolute silence in the home at Bethany! Is there anything analogous to those days in your life? Can God trust you like that, or are you still asking for a visible answer? His silence is the sign that He is bringing you in to a marvelous understanding of Himself. If God has given you a silence, praise Him, He is bringing you into the great run of His purposes. The manifestation of the answer in time is a matter of God's sovereignty. Time is nothing to God.MUH

Reflection Questions

What prayers has God answered after I thought it was too late? How would my prayers and my life be different if I could understand what it means that God is not bounded by time?

IF WE ONLY take as answers those that are visible to our senses, we are in a very elementary condition of grace.IYA

ARE WE MOURNING before God because we have not had an audible response? Mary Magdalene was weeping at the sepulchre—what was she asking for? The dead body of Jesus. Of whom did she ask it? Of Jesus Himself, and she did not know Him! Did Jesus give her what she asked for? He gave her something infinitely grander than she had ever conceived—a risen, living impossible-to-die Lord.[IYA]

Reflection Questions

Am I willing to endure God's silence while He goes about preparing His answer or do I expect Him to give me a progress report every day or so? What does that say about my faith?

WATCH GOD'S WAYS in your life, you will find He is developing you as He does the trees and the flowers, a deep silent working of the God of creation.[DI]

147

EVERY DAY LIVES are passing by us. How much of heaven's inaction have we broken up by our prayers for them? How much of our praying is from the empty spaces round our own hearts and how much from the basis of the redemption, so that we give no thought for ourselves or for others, but only for Jesus Christ?[HGM]

Reflection Questions

Are my prayers so powerful they put heaven in motion or so weak they put heaven to sleep? Do I look forward to getting alone with God every day? How can I make prayer a more joyful experience for myself and for God?

GOD GRANT WE may learn more and more of the profound joy of getting alone with God in the dark of the night and toward the early dawn.[HGM]

Requires Silence

THINK OF THE things you prayed to God about and tried to hold and, because of His love, He dared not let you hold them and they went. For a time you said, "I asked God to give me bread and He gave me a stone"; He did not, and you find today He gave you the bread of life.[IYA]

Reflection Questions

What prayers did God answer in a better way than I expected by not giving me exactly what I prayed for? What things might God be withholding from me for my own good and for the good of His kingdom?

SOME PRAYERS ARE followed by silence because they are wrong, others because they are bigger than we can understand.[IYA]

IT WILL BE a wonderful moment for some of us when we stand before God and find that the prayers we clamored for in early days and imagined were never answered, have been answered in the most amazing way, and that God's silence has been the sign of the answer.[IYA]

Reflection Questions

Am I willing to accept God's silence as the sign of His answer? What might be some of the reasons why God goes about His work so quietly?

IF WE ALWAYS want to be able to point to something and say, "This is the way God answered my prayer," God cannot trust us yet with His silence.[IYA]

AFTER THE SILENCE of God, if we are spiritual and can interpret His silence, we always get the trust in God that knows prayers are answered every time, not some times. The manifestation of the answer in place and time is a mere matter to God's sovereignty.[IYA]

Reflection Questions

About which of my prayers does God seem unusually silent? Am I willing to trust Him to answer it in His way, in His time, and in His place?

PRAYERS WERE OFFERED years ago and God answered the soul with silence; now He is giving the manifestation of the answer in a revelation that we are scarcely able to comprehend.[IYA]

YOU PRAYED THAT you might keep the thing that seemed to make your life as a Christian possible, you asked that it might always be preserved by God, and suddenly the whole thing went to pieces. That was God's answer.[IYA]

Reflection Questions

If I am willing to give God credit for the seemingly good things that happen in my life, should I also give Him credit for the things that seem bad?

REMEMBER THAT JESUS Christ's silences are always signs that He knows we can stand a bigger revelation than we think we can. If He gives you the exact answer, He cannot trust you yet.[IYA]

BE EARNEST AND eager on the line of praying. One wonderful thing about God's stillness in connection with your prayers is that He makes you still, makes you perfectly confident, the contagion of Jesus Christ's stillness gets into you.[IYA]

Reflection Questions

Do I generally stop talking when God is silent or do I talk all the more, trying to fill in the gaps for Him? Do I generally stop moving forward when God is silent or do I plunge on and expect God to keep my pace?

GOD WILL GIVE the blessings we want if we won't go any further, but His silence is the sign that He is bringing us into this marvelous understanding of Himself.[IYA]

O Lord, for greater sweetness and beauty and roundness of character, I pray; for the gift of spiritual energy and full-patienced life toward all and in Your presence. Your sweetness, patience, beauty—manifest them, O Lord. Preserve me from the pattern and print of the age I live in. Today, O Lord, cleanse me from hurry, and keep me purely and calmly Yours. Renew your joy and power in and through me for your glory, keeping me clear and pure for You.[LBP]

Reflection Questions

Have I ever taken the time to compose a beautiful prayer? How can I make more of my prayers an expression of beauty rather than of greed?

O Lord, by your indwelling Spirit knit me together into worship and beauty and holiness. Lord, touch my body and spirit till both are one with You.[LBP]

A Holy Occupation
Requires Simplicity

LET THE WORDS come home to us personally in their New Testament setting. "When you pray, do not use vain repetitions." Our Lord prayed the same prayer, using the same words, three times in the Garden of Gethsemane, and He gave the disciples a form of prayer which He knew would be repeated throughout the Christian centuries; so it cannot be mere repetition or the form of words that he is referring to. The latter half of the verse comes home better for personal purposes—for they think that they shall be heard for their much speaking—that is, Do not rely on your earnestness as the ground for being heard.^{CD Vol. 2}

Reflection Questions

If I had to listen to my own prayers, would I look forward to them with anticipation or dread? If my prayers are so dull they put me to sleep, how might God feel about them?

Requires Simplicity

THE TENDENCY IN prayer to leave ourselves all abroad to the influence of a meeting or of a special season is not scriptural. Prayer is an effort of will, and Jesus Christ instructs us by using the word "ask." "Everyone who asks receives." These words are an amazing revelation of the simplicity with which God would have us pray. The other domains of prayer, the intercession of the Holy Spirit and the intercession of Christ, are nothing to do with us; the effort of our will is to do with us.MFL

Reflection Questions
In what ways do I complicate my prayer life unnecessarily?

AVOID EVERY TENDENCY away from the simplicity of relationship to God in Christ Jesus, and then prayer will be as the breath of the lungs in a healthy body.CD Vol. 2

WE CAN ONLY keep ourselves in the love of God by building up ourselves on our most holy faith and by Holy Spirit-praying, and by nothing else. If we try to fight God's battles with our own weapons and in our own moral resisting power, we shall fail and fail miserably; but if we use the spiritual weapons of implicit trust in God, a simple relationship to Jesus Christ, and responsiveness to the Holy Spirit, we shall never fail.[LG]

Reflection Questions
Which spiritual battles do I fight with my
own weapons rather than with God's?

IF WE STRUGGLE in prayer it is because the enemy is gaining ground. If prayer is simple to us, it is because we have the victory.[IYA]

Requires Simplicity

THROUGH HIS OWN agony in redemption, God has made it as easy to pray as it sounds. There is nothing a rationally minded being can ridicule more easily than prayer. "Praying always"—the unutterable simplicity of it! No panic, no flurry, always at leisure from ourselves on the inside.[IYA]

Reflection Questions

Do I pray more out of panic in response to my circumstances or out of faith in response to God's promises?

WHEN WE PRAY, remember we pray to a Person, "Our Father," not to a tendency; or for the resulting reflex action; and we pray for particular personal needs, which are universal. "Daily bread," "debts," "debtors," "deliverances," and we pray as citizens of a universal spiritual kingdom—"Yours is the kingdom" and the manner is bald, simple but absolutely spiritual.[CD Vol. 2]

WATCH AND PRAY, lest you enter into temptation. The spirit indeed is willing, but the flesh is weak. These words were spoken in the supreme moment of our Lord's agony; we are immensely flippant if we forget that. No words our Lord ever spoke ought to weigh with us more than these words. We are dealing with the sacred simplicity of prayer.[IYA]

Reflection Questions

How does prayer keep me from giving in to temptation?

OUR LORD'S TEACHING about prayer is so amazingly simple but at the same time so amazingly profound that we are apt to miss His meaning. The danger is to water down what Jesus says about prayer and make it mean something more common sense; if it were only common sense, it was not worth His while to say it. The things Jesus says about prayer are supernatural revelation.[OBH]

PRAYER IS SIMPLE, prayer is supernatural, and to anyone not related to our Lord Jesus Christ, prayer is apt to look stupid. It sounds unreasonable to say that God will do things in answer to prayer, yet our Lord said that He would.[IYA]

Reflection Questions

In what ways do I complicate my life because I am unwilling to simply trust God?

TO PUT PRAYER, devotion, obedience, consecration, or any experience, as the means of sanctification is the proof that we are on the wrong line. In sanctification the one reality is the Lord Himself; if you know Him, you will pay no attention to experiences.[PH]

WE HAVE TO live depending on Jesus Christ's wisdom, not on our own. He is the Master, and the problem is His, not ours. We have to use the key He gives us, the key of prayer. Our Lord puts the key into our hands, and we have to learn to pray under His direction. That is the simplicity which He says His Father will bless.[SSY]

Reflection Questions
How does my wisdom differ from God's?

O LORD GOD Almighty, how I long to be centered in You, so completely centered in You that I do not realize it. O speak with power and wisdom and grace and might! O Lord, why cannot I be thrilled in every way by Your goodness—but this is selfishness in desire for feelings of joy. How clearly You have shown me that it is God and God alone who matters.[LBP]

A Holy Occupation
Requires Wonder

OVER AND OVER again God has to teach us how to stand and endure, watching actively and wondering. It is always a wonder when God answers prayer. We hear people say, "We must not say it is wonderful that God answers prayer"; but it is wonderful. It is so wonderful that a great many people believe it impossible. Listen! "Whatever you ask in My name, that I will do." Isn't that wonderful? It is so wonderful that I do not suppose more than half of us really believe it. "Everyone who asks receives." Isn't that wonderful? It is so wonderful that many of us have never even asked God to give us the Holy Spirit because we don't believe He will. "If two of you agree on earth concerning anything that they ask, it will be done for them by My Father in heaven." Isn't that wonderful? It is tremendously wonderful.[IYA]

Reflection Questions
What keeps me from exercising the
wonderful privilege of prayer?

Requires Wonder

IN THIS MANNER, *therefore, pray.* How blessed it is to begin at the beginning, spiritual minors, stripped of our rich and verbal devotional language, and impoverished into receptive teachableness. Let our minds, made fertile by reason of genuine humility, receive the ideas our Lord presents in this familiar pattern prayer; receive in wonder and reverence the simple idea of God's personal relationship to us. Our Father gathers us near Him in the secret place alone with our fears and apprehensions and foolishnesses and aspirations, and He rewards us. When we talk about the fatherhood of God, let us remember that the Lord Jesus is the exclusive way to the Father. That is not an idea to be inferred, but to be received: "No one comes to the Father, except through Me."CD Vol. 2

Reflection Questions
In what ways do I try to gain God's favor other than through Jesus?

WHEN THROUGH JESUS Christ we are rightly related to God, we learn to watch and wait, and wait wonderingly. "I wonder how God will answer this prayer." "I wonder how God will answer the prayer the Holy Spirit is praying in me." "I wonder what glory God will bring to Himself out of the strange perplexities I am in." "I wonder what new turn His providence will take in manifesting Himself in my ways."[IYA]

Reflection Questions

When my circumstances are peculiar or distressing do I wait with wonder on God or chastise Him for allowing them?

PRAYER IS NOT a question of altering things externally, but of working wonders in a man's disposition. When you pray, things remain the same, but you begin to be different.[IYA]

Requires Wonder

IT IS A mistake to interpret prayer on the natural instead of on the spiritual line, to say that because prayer brings us peace and joy and makes us feel better, therefore it is a divine thing. This is the mere accident or effect of prayer; there is no real God-given revelation in it. This is the God-given revelation: that when we are born again of the Spirit of God and indwelt by the Holy Spirit, He intercedes for us with a tenderness and an understanding akin to the Lord Jesus Christ and akin to God; that is, He expresses the unutterable for us.[IYA]

Reflection Questions
In what areas do I assume that my feelings about an issue are God's feelings? What should I trust instead of my feelings?

PRAYER IS NOT logical, it is a mysterious moral working of the Holy Spirit.[CD Vol. 2]

GOD MADE A tremendous promise to Abram, and Abram thought out the best way of helping God fulfill His promise and did the wisest thing he knew according to flesh and blood common-sense reasoning. But for thirteen years God never spoke to him until every possibility of his relying on his own intelligent understanding was at an end. Then God came to him and said, "I am Almighty God"—El Shaddai—"Walk before me, and be blameless." Over and over again God has to teach us how to stand and endure, watching actively and wonderingly.[IYA]

Reflection Questions
What promise of God am I trying to fulfill in my own strength?

HOW GOD WORKS in answer to prayer is a mystery that logic cannot penetrate, but that He does work in answer to prayer is gloriously true.[SSY]

THE ONLY SANE Being who ever trod this earth was Jesus Christ, because in Him the actual and the real were one. Jesus Christ does not stand first in the actual world. He stands first in the real world; that is why the natural man does not bother his head about Him. When we are born from above we begin to see the actual things in the light of the real.[SSM]

Reflection Questions

How well am I doing at learning to see things in the natural realm in light of the spiritual realm? How does prayer help?

IF WE ONLY look for results in the earthlies when we pray, we are ill-taught. A praying saint performs far more havoc among the unseen forces of darkness than we have the slightest notion of.[BP]

THE PRAYERS OF the saints either enable or disable God in the performance of His wonders. The majority of us in praying for the will of God to be done say, "In God's good time," meaning "in my bad time"; consequently there is no silence in heaven produced by our prayers, no results, no performance.[HGM]

Reflection Questions

In what ways might my prayers be disabling God in the performance of His wonders?

O LORD, I do praise You that in Christ Jesus it is all of You, it is mercy and loving kindness, graciousness and wonders all along the way. I would be sensitive to You and Your doings, and Christ-like in my gratitude. Be in and out among us this day in power; touch every one of us.[LBP]

A Holy Occupation
Requires Work

OVER AND OVER again men have turned to prayer, not in the extreme of weakness, but of limitation; whenever a man gets beyond the limit he unconsciously turns to God. Eliphaz claimed to know exactly where Job was, and Bildad claimed the same thing. Job was hurt, and these men tried to heal him with platitudes. The place for the comforter is not that of one who preaches, but of the comrade who says nothing and prays to God about the matter. The biggest thing you can do for those who are suffering is not to talk platitudes, not to ask questions, but to get into contact with God, and the "greater work" will be done by prayer.[BFB]

Reflection Questions

What person needs the comfort and assurance of my presence rather than the annoyance of my pious platitudes?

Requires Work

THANK GOD FOR all the marvelous organization there
is in Christian work, for medical missions and finely educated missionaries, for aggressive work in every shape
and form; but the key is not in any of our organizations,
the key lies exactly to our hand by our Lord's instruc-
tion, "Pray."IYA

Reflection Questions
What missionaries will I
pray for today?

WE HAVE NOT the remotest conception of what is
done by our prayers, nor have we the right to try and
examine and understand it; all we know is that Jesus
Christ laid all stress on prayer. "And greater works than
these will he do, because I go to My Father. And whatever you ask in My name, that I will do."BFB

HAVE WE ALSO to do greater works than Jesus did? Certainly we have, if our Lord's words mean anything, they mean that; and the great basis of prayer is to realize that we must take our orders form our Master. He made prayer not a sentiment nor a devotion, but the work to which He called us.[IYA]

Reflection Questions
When was the last time I "worked"
at prayer?

NOT ONLY IS prayer the work, but prayer is the way by which fruit is preserved. Our Lord puts prayer as the means to fruit-producing and fruit-preserving work; but remember, it is prayer based on His agony, not on our agony.[IYA]

Requires Work

SO MANY OF us put prayer and work and consecration in place of the working of God; we make ourselves the workers. God is the Worker, we work out what He works in. Spirituality is what God is after, not religiosity.[IWP]

Reflection Questions

In what ways am I beginning to understand the difference between spirituality and religiosity?

THE "GREATER WORKS" are done by prayer because prayer is the exercise of the essential character of the life of God in us.[PH]

THERE IS NOTHING thrilling about a laboring man's work, but it is the laboring man who makes the conceptions of the genius possible; and it is the laboring saint who makes the conceptions of his Master possible. You labor at prayer and results happen all the time from His standpoint.ᴹᵁᴴ

Reflection Questions

Am I willing to be a common laborer for Jesus or am I like James and John, two of Jesus' disciples, who were striving to win a higher position? Is there any such thing for believers?

PRAY THE LORD *of the harvest to send out laborers into His harvest.* This is the key to the whole problem of Christian work. It is simple in words, but amazingly profound, because our Lord Jesus Christ said it.ᴵʸᴬ

UNTIL WE ARE born from above, prayer with us is honestly nothing more than a mere exercise; but in all our Lord's teaching and in His own personal life, as well as in the emphasis laid on prayer by the Holy Spirit after He had gone, prayer is regarded as the work.[PR]

Reflection Questions
What am I accomplishing through the work of prayer? Have I received proper training for a career of prayer? How and where can I learn more about it?

THE PLACE OF prayer in the New Testament is just this one of severe technical training in which spiritual sympathies are sustained in unsecular strength.[CD Vol. 2]

IT IS THE vital necessity for Christians to think along the lines on which they pray. The philosophy of prayer is that prayer is the work.^{CD Vol. 2}

Reflection Questions

Do I pray out of thoughtfulness or habit? What can I do to get my mind involved as well as my mouth?

LORD, BLESSED BE Your name, I adore You for all that You have enabled me to do in realizing You. Lord, increase my certainty that You do take me up into Your consciousness, and not that I take You into mine. O Lord, that I might be God-centered in every way—God-centered in thought and word and deed, and not distracted from that Center. Bless us all today, garrison minds and hearts from vague fancies and inordinate affections and from false emotions and specters of the imagination and keep us wholesomely Yours.^{LBP}

A Holy Occupation
Requires Worship

WORSHIP AND INTERCESSION must go together, the one is impossible without the other. Intercession means that we rouse ourselves up to get the mind of Christ about the one for whom we pray. Too often instead of worshiping God, we construct statements as to how prayer works. Are we worshiping or are we in dispute with God—"I don't see how You are going to do it." This is a sure sign that we are not worshiping. When we lose sight of God we become hard and dogmatic. We hurl our own petitions at God's throne and dictate to Him as to what we wish Him to do. We do not worship God, nor do we seek to form the mind of Christ. If we are hard towards God, we will become hard towards other people.^{MUH}

Reflection Questions
What does my attitude toward others tell me about my relationship with God?

Requires Worship

ARE WE LIVING in such a vital relationship to our fellow men that we do the work of intercession as the Spirit-taught children of God? Begin with the circumstances we are in—our homes, our businesses, our country, the present crisis as it touches us and others—are these things crushing us? Are they badgering us out of the presence of God and leaving us no time for worship? Then let us call a halt and get into such a living relationship with God that our relationship to others may be maintained on the line of intercession whereby God works His marvels.ᴹᵁᴴ

Reflection Questions

Do I allow my relationships with others to affect my relationship with God or do I allow my relationship with God to affect my relationships with others?

THE TENDENCY NOWADAYS is to worship prayer; stress is put on nights of prayer and the difficulty and cost of prayer. It is not prayer that is strenuous, but the overcoming of our own laziness. If we make the basis of prayer our effort and agony and nights of prayer, we mistake the basis of prayer. The basis of prayer is not what it costs us, but what it costs God to enable us to pray.[IYA]

Reflection Questions
Do I worship prayer
or pray worshipfully?

BE THE ONE who worships God and who lives in holy relationship to Him. Get into the real work of intercession, and remember it is a work, a work that taxes every power; but a work which has no snare. Preaching the gospel has a snare; intercessory prayer has none.[MUH]

Requires Worship

THE REASON PRAYER is so important is, first of all, because our Lord told us that prayer is the most mighty factor He has put into our hands, and second, because of the personal presence of the Holy Spirit in the day in which we live. We receive our knowledge of the Holy Spirit not by experience first, but by the testimony of the Lord Jesus Christ. The testimony of Jesus Christ regarding the Holy Spirit is that He is here, and the real living experience the Holy Spirit works in us is that all His emphasis is laid on glorifying our Lord Jesus Christ. We know the Holy Spirit first by the testimony of Jesus, and then by the conscious enjoyment of His presence.[IYA]

Reflection Questions
Do I know what it means
to enjoy God's presence?

PRAYER IS THE instrument of the life of worship, it is not worship itself.[CD Vol. 2]

BEWARE OF OUTSTRIPPING God by your very longing to do His will. We run ahead of Him in a thousand and one activities, consequently we get so burdened with persons and with difficulties that we do not worship God, we do not intercede.^{MUH}

Reflection Questions
How will I pray and how will I behave today in response to the assurance of God's sovereignty?

O LORD, THIS morning disperse every mist, and shine clear and strong and invigoratingly. Forgive my tardiness, it takes me so long to awaken to some things. Lord God Omniscient, give me wisdom this day to worship and work aright and be well-pleasing to You. Lord, interpret Yourself to me more and more in fullness and beauty. Dark and appalling are the clouds of war and wickedness and we know not where to turn, but, Lord God, You reign.^{IYA}

Index of Selections

Index of Subjects

187

Note to the Reader

The publisher invites you to share your response to the message of this book by writing Discovery House Publishers, P.O. Box 3566, Grand Rapids, MI 49501, U.S.A. or by calling 1-800-653-8333. For information about other Discovery House publications, contact us at the same address and phone number.